THE STENCIL COLLECTION
Fruits & Flowers
Katrina Hall

Spring Lilies & Crab Apples

Chinese Pomegranates

Paisley Harvest

Provençal Figs & Clematis

Passion Fruit & Flowers

Cottage Garden

INTRODUCING STENCILLING

Once you begin stencilling you will be amazed at the wonderful results you can obtain quite easily and without spending a great deal of money. This book introduces six themed projects and provides ready-to-use stencils that can be used with numerous variations in design – just follow the step-by-step features and simple instructions. With very little paint and only a few pieces of equipment you can achieve stunning results. Have fun!

BASIC MATERIALS

Paints and Decorative Finishes
Emulsion paint
Water-based stencil paint
Oil sticks
Acrylic paints (bottles and tubes)
Specialist paints (for fabrics, ceramics, glass etc)
Spray paints
Metallic acrylic artists' colours (gold, silver etc)
Silver and gold art flow pens
Bronze powders (various metallics)
Gilt wax

Brushes and Applicators
Art brushes (variety of sizes)
Stencil brushes (small, medium and large)
Sponge applicators
Mini-roller and tray

Other Equipment
Set square
Blotting paper
Scissors or scalpel (or craft knife)
Roll of lining paper (for practising)
Eraser
Soft pencil
Fine-tip permanent pen
Chalk or Chalkline and powdered chalk
Long rigid ruler
Tape measure
Plumbline
Spirit level
Low-tack masking tape
Spray adhesive
Tracing paper
Paint dishes or palettes
Cloths
Kitchen roll
White spirit
Stencil plastic or card
Cotton buds
Methylated spirits

CUTTING OUT STENCILS
The stencils at the back of the book are all designed to use separately or together to create many different pattern combinations. Cut along the dotted lines of the individual stencils and make sure you transfer the reference code onto each one with a permanent pen. Carefully remove the cut-out pieces of the stencil. Apply 50 mm (2 in) strips of tracing paper around the edges using masking tape; this will help to prevent smudging paint onto your surface.

REPAIRING STENCILS
Stencils may become damaged and torn from mishandling, or if the cutouts have not been removed carefully, but they are easy to repair. Keeping the stencil perfectly flat, cover both sides of the tear with masking tape. Then carefully remove any excess tape with a scalpel.

GETTING STARTED

DUPLICATING STENCILS

Stencil plastic (Mylar) can be used; or card wiped over with linseed oil, which left to dry will harden and make the surface waterproof. Place the cut-out stencil on top. Trace around carefully with a permanent pen inside the cut-out shapes. Cut along the lines with a scalpel and remove the pieces. You may prefer to trace on top of the design, then transfer your tracing onto card.

MAKING A SPONGE APPLICATOR

Sponging your stencil is one of the easiest methods, but you may prefer to use a stencil brush, especially for fine detail. Using a piece of upholstery foam or very dense bath sponge, cut pieces 12–50 mm (1/2–2 in) wide and approximately 50 mm (2 in) long. Hold the four corners together and secure with tape to form a pad. You can also round off the ends with scissors or a scalpel and trim to a smooth finish. The small-ended applicators can be used for tiny, intricate patterns.

HOW TO USE WATER-BASED PAINT

Water-based paints are easy and economical to use and have the advantage of drying quickly. For professional-looking stencils, do not load your sponge or brush too heavily or you will not achieve a soft, shaded finish. Paint that is too watery will seep under the stencil edges and smudge. If the paint is too heavy you will obtain a heavy block effect rather than the soft stippling you require.

LOOKING AFTER STENCILS

Stencils have a long life if cared for correctly. Before cleaning make sure you remove any tape or tracing paper that has been added. Remove any excess paint before it dries, and wipe the stencil with a damp cloth every time you use it. If water or acrylic paint has dried and hardened, soften it with water and ease it off gently with a scalpel. Then use a small amount of methylated spirits on a cloth to remove the rest. An oil-based paint can simply be removed by wiping over the stencil with white spirit on a cloth. Stencils should be dried thoroughly before storing flat between sheets of greaseproof paper.

HOW TO USE OIL STICKS

Oil sticks may seem expensive, but in fact go a long way. They take longer to dry, allowing you to blend colours very effectively. Oil sticks are applied with a stencil brush and you need to have a different brush for each colour. Break the seal as instructed on the stick and rub a patch of the colour onto a palette, allowing space to blend colours. As the stencil sticks dry slowly, you need to lift the stencil off cleanly, and replace to continue the pattern.

PRACTISING PAINTING STENCILS

Roll out some lining paper onto a table and select the stencil you wish to practise with. Using spray adhesive, lightly spray the back of your stencil and place it into position on the paper. Prepare your paint on a palette. Dab your sponge or brush into the paint and offload excess paint onto scrap paper. Apply colour over the stencil in a light coat to create an even stippled effect. You can always stencil on a little more paint if a stronger effect is needed, but if you over apply it in the first place it is very difficult to remove. Keep separate sponges for different colours.

PLANNING YOUR DESIGN

Before starting to stencil take time to plan your design. Decide where you want to use the patterns, then work out how to position the stencils so that the design will fit around obstacles such as doorways and corners. The techniques shown here will help you to undertake the job with a systematic approach.

PUTTING PATTERN PIECES TOGETHER

1 Before you apply your design, stencil a sample onto lining paper. Mark the centre and baseline of the design on the paper and put together your pattern pieces. You can then work out the size of the design, how it will fit into the space available and the distance required between repeats.

2 You can avoid stencilling around a corner by working out the number of pattern repeats needed, and allowing extra space either between repeats or within the pattern. Creating vertical lines through the pattern will allow you to stretch it evenly.

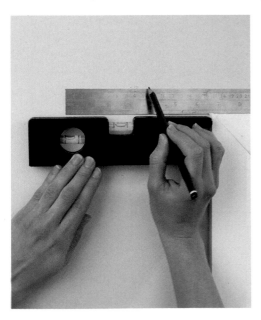

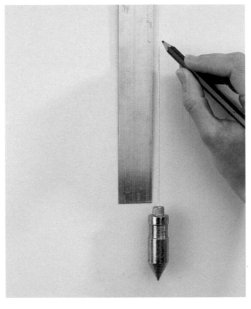

MARKING BASELINES AND HORIZONTAL LINES

Select your stencil area, and take a measure from the ceiling, doorframe, window or edging, bearing in mind the depth of your stencil. Using a spirit level, mark out a horizontal line. You can then extend this by using a chalkline or long ruler with chalk or soft pencil.

MARKING VERTICAL LINES

If you need to work out the vertical position for a stencil, hang a plumbline above the stencilling area and use a ruler to draw a vertical line with chalk or a soft pencil. You will need to use this method when creating an all-over wallpaper design.

FIXING THE STENCIL INTO PLACE

Lightly spray the back of the stencil with spray adhesive, then put it in position and smooth it down carefully. You can use low-tack masking tape if you prefer, but take care not to damage the surface to be stencilled; keep the whole stencil flat to prevent paint seeping underneath.

MARKING THE STENCIL FOR A PATTERN REPEAT

Attach a border of tracing paper to each edge of the stencil. Position the next pattern and overlap the tracing paper onto the previous design, tracing over the edge of it. By matching the tracing with the previous pattern as you work along you will be able to align and repeat the stencil at the same intervals.

COPING WITH CORNERS

Stencil around corners after you have finished the rest of the design, having measured to leave the correct space for the corner pattern before you do so. Then bend the stencil into the corner and mask off one side of it. Stencil the open side and allow the paint to dry, then mask off this half and stencil the other part to complete the design.

MASKING OFF PART OF A STENCIL

Use low-tack masking tape to mask out small or intricate areas of stencil. You can also use ordinary masking tape, but remove excess stickiness first by peeling it on and off your skin or a cloth once or twice. To block off inside shapes and large areas, cut out pieces of tracing paper to the appropriate size and fix them on top with spray adhesive.

MITRING STENCIL PATTERNS

1 When you are stencilling a continuous pattern and need to make a corner, mask off the stencil by marking a 45-degree angle at both ends of the stencil with a permanent pen. Mask along this line with a piece of masking tape or tracing paper.

2 Make sure the baselines of the stencil on both sides of the corner are the same distance from the edge, and that they cross at the corner. Put the diagonal end of the stencil right into the corner and apply the paint. Turn the stencil sideways to align the other diagonal end of the stencil and turn the corner.

PAINT EFFECTS

CHOOSING COLOURS

Take care to choose appropriate colours to create the effect you want. Stencil a practice piece onto paper and try a variation of colours to ensure you are pleased with the result. Different colours can make a design look entirely different. Use spray adhesive to fix your practice paper onto the surface on which you wish to produce the design so that you can assess its effect before applying the stencil.

APPLYING WATER-BASED COLOURS

Water-based paint dries quickly, so it tends to layer rather than blend. It is best applied by using a swirling movement or gently dabbing, depending on the finished effect you wish to create. Once you have applied a light base colour, you can add a darker edge for shading. Alternatively, leave some of the stencil bare and add a different tone to that area to obtain a shaded or highlighted appearance.

BLENDING OIL-STICK COLOURS

Oil sticks mix together smoothly and are perfect for blending colours. Place the colours separately on your palette and mix them with white to obtain a variety of tones or blend them together to create new colours. You can also blend by applying one coat into another with a stippling motion while stencilling. Blending looks most effective when applying a pale base coat, then shading on top with a darker colour.

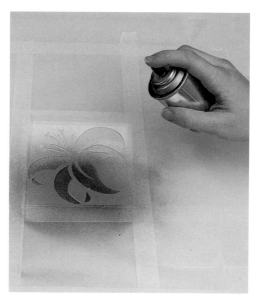

HIGHLIGHTING

A simple way to add highlighting to your design is first to paint in your stencil in a light tone of your main colour, then carefully lift the stencil and move it down a fraction. Then stencil in a darker shade; this leaves the highlighted areas around the top edges of the pattern.

GILDING

After painting your stencil use gold to highlight the edges. Load a fine art brush with gold acrylic paint and carefully outline the top edges of the pattern. Use one quick brush stroke for each pattern repeat, keeping in the same direction. Other methods are to blow bronze powder onto the wet paint, draw around the pattern with a gold flow pen, or smudge on gilt wax cream, then buff to a high sheen.

APPLYING SPRAY PAINTS

Spray paints are ideal on glass, wood, metal, plastic and ceramic surfaces. They are quick to apply and fast drying, but cannot be blended, although you can achieve subtle shaded effects. Apply the paint in several thin coats. Mask off a large area around the design to protect it from the spray, which tends to drift. Try to use sprays out of doors or in a well-ventilated area. Some spray paints are non-toxic, making them ideal for children's furniture.

DIFFERENT SURFACES

BARE WOOD

Rub the wood surface down to a smooth finish. Then fix the stencil in place and paint with a thin base coat of white, so that the stencil colours will stand out well when applied. Leave the stencil in place and allow to dry thoroughly, then apply your stencil colours in the normal way. When completely dry you can apply a coat of light wax or varnish to protect your stencil.

PAINTED WOOD

If you are painting wood or medium-density fibreboard (MDF) prior to stencilling, seal it with a coat of acrylic primer before adding a base coat of emulsion or acrylic paint. If the base coat is dark, stencil a thin coat of white paint on top. Apply your stencil and, if required, protect with a coat of clear varnish when it is completely dry.

FABRIC

Use special fabric paint for stencilling on fabric and follow the manufacturer's instructions carefully. Place card or blotting paper behind the fabric while working and keep the material taut. If you are painting a dark fabric, best results are achieved by stencilling first with white or a lighter shade. Heat seal the design following the manufacturer's instructions.

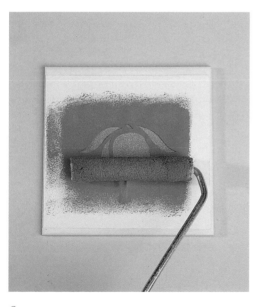

CERAMICS

Use special ceramic paints to work directly onto glazed ceramic tiles, and unglazed ceramics such as terracotta. Make sure all surfaces are clean, so that the stencils can be fixed easily. Apply the paint with a brush, sponge, spray or mini-roller. Ceramic paints are durable and washable, and full manufacturer's instructions are given on the container.

GLASS

Before applying the stencil make sure the glass is clean, spray on a light coat of adhesive and place the stencil in position. Spray on water-based or ceramic paint, remove the stencil and allow to dry. If you wish to stencil drinking glasses, use special non-toxic and water-resistant glass paints. An etched-glass look with stencils on windows, doors and mirrors can be achieved with a variety of materials.

PAINTED SURFACES

Stencils can be applied to surfaces painted with matt, satin or vinyl silk emulsion, oil scumble glazes, acrylic glazes and varnishes, and to matt wallpaper. If you wish to decorate a gloss surface, stencil first with an acrylic primer, leave to dry and then stencil the colours on top. Surfaces to be stencilled need to be smooth so that the stencil can lay flat.

PAINT COLOUR GUIDE

White   Lime green   Dark green

PAINTING THE BORDER

1 First paint your wall with apple green emulsion.

2 Carefully mark out the border using a spirit level and mask off the stencilling area with low-tack tape or string pinned at intervals.

3 Gently spray the backs of the stencils with spray adhesive, leave for a few minutes so the glue is not too sticky, then start to put them in position.

4 Position your stencils randomly, trying not to repeat the same motif next to itself. Place them at varying angles – even sideways or upside down. Reposition them until you are happy with the pattern.

SPRING LILIES & CRAB APPLES

D elicate white lilies are traditionally associated with modesty and purity, but they make an effective contrast with the familiar culinary properties of acid green crab apples. To create an instant impression of peace and harmony you could use any of these stencils in different combinations. There are no hard and fast rules, so move the stencils as your space dictates. Transform a plain kitchen wall, as here, or perhaps trail the shapes over your garden furniture and tubs.

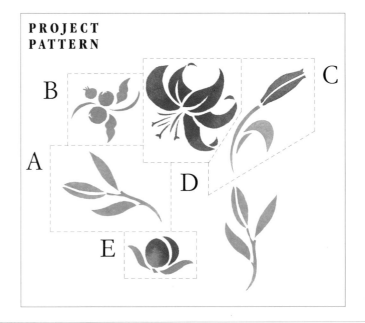

PROJECT PATTERN

B   C   A   D   E

PAINTING LIGHT ON DARK
It is usual to start with a light background and paint darker coloured stencils. Here the combination of light on dark and dark on light adds to the depth of the design. To work with white use a clean sponge and dry stencil.

FADING FOR AN AGED LOOK
A fresco effect can be achieved by fading colours into the background. In this way the end result will not look so contrived and the stencilled image will look as if it has been on the wall for years.

BALANCING THE DESIGN
Placing the stencils randomly may seem an easy option, but it requires careful planning. Take the time to stand back and see that the weight of the design is level. Fiddle with the different elements in the empty spaces until one fits.

SPRING LILIES & CRAB APPLES VARIATIONS

Instead of the cool effect of the lime green and white combination I used on the kitchen wall, try a variation. How about burgundy lilies with more muted green crab apples, for example? Use the lilies on their own or leave the crab apples cooking in rows. For a more sophisticated setting try the designs in a dining room.

LILY FLOWERS BORDER (STENCIL D)

CRAB-APPLE FRIEZE IN TWO COLOURS (STENCIL B)

ONE TONE BUD AND SPRIG REPEAT (STENCILS A AND C)

LILY FLOWER AND CRAB-APPLE BORDER (STENCILS B AND D)

CRAB-APPLES AND LILY BUD BORDER (STENCILS A, B AND E)

**LEFT: SIMPLE
LINKING SPRIGS**
(STENCIL **C**)

**ABOVE: LARGE
CRAB-APPLE
BORDER**
(STENCIL **E**)

**LEFT: TWISTING
CRAB-APPLE
FRIEZE**
(STENCIL **B**)

BOLD FLOWER PATTERN
(STENCIL **D**)

LILY ART DECO DESIGN
(STENCIL **C**)

**LILY FLOWER AND
BUD REPEAT**
(STENCILS **A** AND **D**)

SIMPLE LINKING BUDS
(STENCIL **A**)

PAINT COLOUR GUIDE

Bright blue

DECORATING THE BATH

1 Paint the side of the bath with a couple of coats of white paint.

2 Position the solid pomegranate (stencil E) first, then put in a leaf and flower, making sure they do not touch. Then position the more delicate fruit (stencil C) at an angle. Follow this with a couple of flowers and a leaf.

3 Trace the pattern to make the repeating process simpler. Slide the stencils under the trace to the right position and remove it to paint. Draw the position of the previous repeat onto the tracing paper to align the repeats correctly.

CHINESE POMEGRANATES

The familiar Chinese willow pattern inspired this design of pomegranates with flowers and leaves, and its cool blue and white colour scheme is particularly suitable for a bathroom. The motifs can be used throughout the room – on the walls, the laundry basket, the bath panels and even the windows. They make a dramatic-looking design when positioned closely together to create a border. Individual elements could also be used to simulate hand-blocked wallpaper using a symmetrical pattern.

PROJECT PATTERN

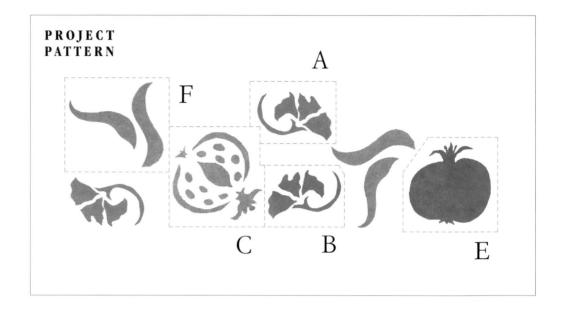

SQUARING UP

Rather than spending hours putting plumb lines etc. on the bath, use masking tape to stick a mini spirit level on the side of the bath. Then you can align and square up your stencil with the level. This makes repositioning much easier.

REVERSING THE COLOUR SCHEME

If you are working with a two colour scheme, it is fun to paint the combination somewhere in the room the opposite way round. Dramatically contrasting colours work well, but use the technique with similar tones for a more subtle look.

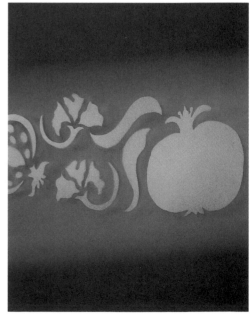

STENCILLING ON WINDOWS

A lovely finish to the scheme can be achieved, especially in bathrooms, if you take the design onto the windows. Mark off the area around the stencil with newspaper and gently spray clear or white spray – this gives a frosted or etched look.

CHINESE POMEGRANATES VARIATIONS

Experiment in your bathroom with a different interpretation of the pomegranate design using aquatints of turquoise and cobalt. Ring the changes with a variation along the same theme. Choosing the right paint for the surface is always tricky. If you want to stencil an uneven surface such as wicker, use a spray paint. Spray evenly using thin coats, to keep the edges of the image well defined.

TWISTING POMEGRANATE FLOWERS (STENCIL **B**)

WHOLE POMEGRANATE BORDER (STENCIL **E**)

LEAVES REPEAT (STENCIL **F**)

POMEGRANATE BORDER (STENCIL **C**)

FLOATING LEAVES
(STENCILS **D** AND **F**)

WHOLE POMEGRANATE AND FLOWERS REPEAT (STENCILS A, B AND E)

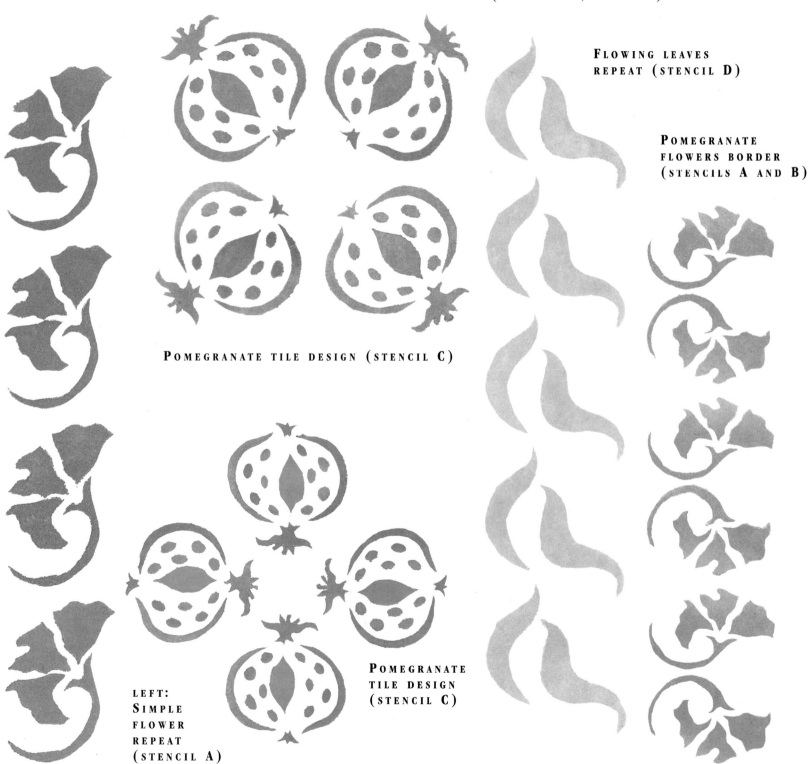

FLOWING LEAVES
REPEAT (STENCIL D)

POMEGRANATE
FLOWERS BORDER
(STENCILS A AND B)

POMEGRANATE TILE DESIGN (STENCIL C)

POMEGRANATE
TILE DESIGN
(STENCIL C)

LEFT:
SIMPLE
FLOWER
REPEAT
(STENCIL A)

PASSION FRUIT & FLOWERS

Here is an easy way to transform a seemingly boring flat wall or hallway. Simply divide it along the traditional dado position and stencil a border. Paint the two areas in contrasting tones to create a wonderful backdrop for these rambling, elegant passion fruit and flowers in lilac, green and burgundy. These motifs look just as effective if applied in a random manner rather than regularly repeated, giving the finished image a more individual, hand-painted look.

PAINT COLOUR GUIDE

Olive green   Lilac   Burgundy

PAINTING A DADO DESIGN

1 Paint the top of the wall in a light stone colour. Use a spirit level to place a horizontal line of low-tack masking tape along the wall, then paint the lower half in a darker colour.

2 Position the two leaf motifs (stencils A and C) so that part of them cross over the two colours.

3 Finally, put in the flower (stencil D) and fruit (stencil B). This can be done by eye or by drawing in the edge of the previous stencil on the card being used to calculate the exact repeat position.

PROJECT PATTERN

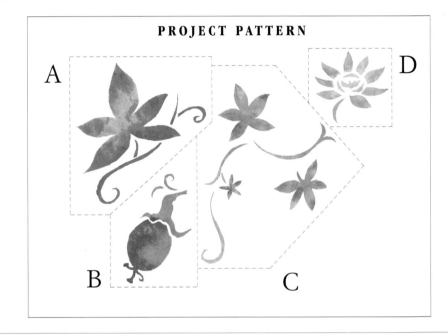

POSITIONING THE REPEAT
When you first position your stencil, draw a line with a permanent marker on the stencil where the stencil is cut by the line of the wall to mark the repeat position. This will make the repeat easier to align.

PAINTING THE LEAVES
Keep some of the leaves totally green and add tinges of other colours on the corners of the stencil to give a more flowing feeling.

PROTECTING THE SURFACE
You could also paint the stencil with the dark colour on the light background and vice versa. If your stencil goes over both backgrounds, put a piece of card on one half for protection and then paint. Repeat the process on the second half.

PASSION FRUIT & FLOWERS VARIATIONS

Experiment with earthy, autumnal colours as an alternative to the fresh summery tones I used for the dado decoration. With their tendrils and abundant fruits and flowers these passion fruit stencils can be used to create a 'growing' image. Make sure that you undulate the stencils to maintain the sense of movement. Blend the tints of the ripening fruit or keep to a single colour.

FRUIT MEDALLION DESIGN (STENCIL B)

LARGE LEAF REPEAT (STENCIL A)

LEAVES AND FRUIT PATTERN (STENCILS B AND C)

REVERSED FRUITS FRIEZE (STENCIL B)

LARGE LEAF BORDER (STENCIL A)

DANGLING FRUIT REPEAT (STENCIL B)

**TWISTED LEAF AND
FLOWER BORDER
(STENCILS C AND D)**

**TRAILING LEAVES
AND TENDRILS
(STENCIL C)**

**FLOWER FRIEZE
(STENCIL D)**

**SIMPLE FLOWER REPEAT
(STENCIL D)**

PAINT COLOUR GUIDE

Damson   Scarlet   Gold

DECORATING THE WARDROBE

1 Paint the wardrobe with white emulsion, then loosely apply a wash of yellow ochre emulsion and water on top.

2 The side panel stencil is a simple 180-degree turn of the same shape (stencil A) – once you have stencilled the first image turn the card upside down and position the second. Use a permanent marker to indicate the edge of the previous stencil for an identical repeat.

3 For the main panel arrange the cards in the desired order, then trace the pattern. Draw the edge of the wardrobe on the tracing so that you can move the pattern down easily. Stick the top edge of the tracing to the wardrobe and lift it up and down to put the stencils in place.

PAISLEY HARVEST

There is an Indian theme to this design of opulent pears and stylized flowers combined with exotic paisley-shaped leaves. The flowers are loosely based on an Indian jasmine and the paisley shape is reputed to have originated from Kashmir. I used rich colours of deep red, damson and gold to convey the essence of Indian culture. Wood is a suitable surface for this Eastern transformation, and gold, with its jewel-like qualities, serves to enhance the design and highlight the shapes.

Protect your stencilling by applying a good acrylic or polyurethane varnish.

PROJECT PATTERN

A

ADDING DEPTH
If you want to create a dense layer of paint, do not overflood the stencil in one layer. Aim for a build-up of thin layers until you gain the required look.

BRUSHING ON HIGHLIGHTS
Hand finishing stencils with a brush gives a wonderful individuality to the design. Either leave the stencil on as a guide and outline a shape or, if you are feeling brave, simply paint on the detail.

SPONGING ON HIGHLIGHTS
Highlights in metallic paints add instant impact. Wait for the initial coat of paint to dry. Then carefully reposition the stencil and work from the outside of the shape, rubbing the sponge gently inwards to leave a faded and uneven edge.

PAISLEY HARVEST VARIATIONS

I decorated the wardrobe with the colours associated with the region of Kashmir – deep reds, damson and gold – but you could also use the riot of iridescent colour found in Rajasthan. Fuchsia pink, yellow ochre and scarlet are reminiscent of the festival of Holi, where teenagers shower each other with brilliant cerise dye powder. So be brave – use bright colours for maximum impact.

If you prefer the more muted look of faded frescoes, use soft hues, gently merging the edges into the background.

ENTWINED LEAF DESIGN
(STENCIL A)

SIMPLE LEAF EDGING (STENCIL D)

LARGE PEARS BORDER (STENCIL F)

FLOWER AND SEEDHEADS REPEAT (STENCIL C)

SMALL PEARS
AND FOLIAGE
REPEAT
(STENCILS B,
D AND E)

FLOWER AND FOLIAGE REPEAT (STENCILS D AND C)

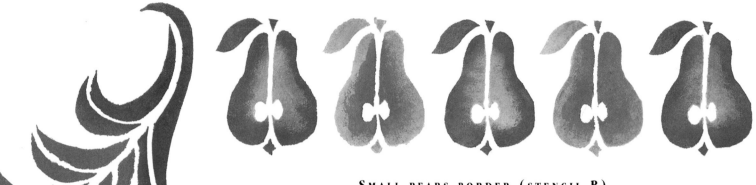

SMALL PEARS BORDER (STENCIL B)

ABOVE: LARGE PEAR AND FOLIAGE MOTIF (STENCILS D, E AND F)

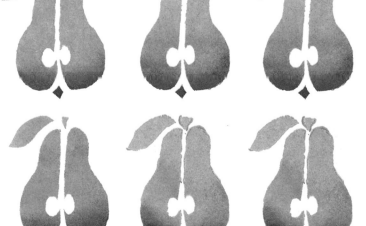

PEAR MOTIF DESIGN (STENCIL B)

CURLING LEAF REPEAT (STENCIL A)

PROVENÇAL FIGS & CLEMATIS

The balmy atmosphere of the South of France is conjured up by this attractive combination of luscious figs and the stately appearance of large clematis blooms. Earthy colours of dark terracotta, purple, olive and cream epitomize autumn in Provence. Create a warm and rustic look on anything from blanket boxes to archways, study walls to kitchen cabinets. The trailing nature of the clematis plant, with its star-shaped flowers and entwining tendrils, particularly lends itself to floors.

PAINT COLOUR GUIDE

Deep purple	Terracotta
Olive green	Golden cream
Dark brown	

PAINTING THE FLOOR PATTERN

1 First whitewash the floorboards with a 50–50 mix of water and white emulsion. Build up in layers until you have the desired effect.

2 Position the stencil cards on the floor. Try and keep the pattern looking like it is growing so that it engulfs the surface.

3 Alternate the leaves with tendrils, flowers and figs totally at random. If you come across a good combination, repeat it, but at a good distance from the first so that you achieve a natural-looking effect.

Floors should be finished off with a couple of coats of varnish.

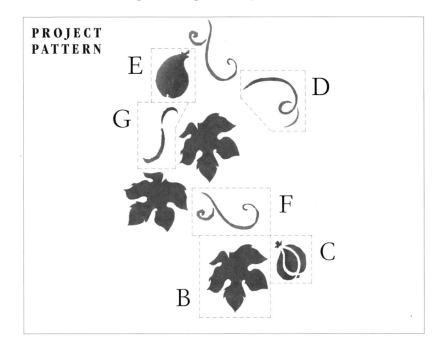

PROJECT PATTERN

MOTTLED LEAVES
To achieve a mottled look within each element, dab the stencil with one colour, let it dry for a moment, then sponge a different colour on top. This gives a wonderful uneven effect.

SHADING THE FIGS
Create graduated shading by blending into the first colour while it is still wet. Start with the darker colour, but do not put it quite as far as you ultimately want it to go. Then work back towards this with the lighter colour.

TACKLING CORNERS
Work around corners in as flowing a manner as possible. Sometimes it helps to put an element such as a tendril in the corner to give definition. Stand back as you progress to check you are maintaining the feeling of movement.

PROVENÇAL FIGS & CLEMATIS VARIATIONS

As a contrast to the ripening purple figs I used as a floor decoration, try a more subdued colour scheme. For a lighter effect combine olive green figs with creamy white clematis blooms. Perhaps you could paint the design growing along the floor over the skirting board and up the wall. The motifs could also be used as all-over hand-painted 'wallpaper' designs.

FIGS AND TENDRILS BORDER (STENCILS C AND F)

LEAF BLOCK BORDER (STENCIL B)

LEFT: SIMPLE RIBBON REPEAT (STENCIL G)

CLEMATIS REPEAT (STENCIL A)

CLEMATIS AND CURLING TENDRILS BORDER (STENCILS A AND D)

SIMPLE FIG BORDER (STENCIL E)

TENDRIL EDGING (STENCIL F)

LEAF, RIBBON AND FIG PATTERN (STENCILS B, C AND G)

FIGS AND CURLING TENDRILS (STENCILS C, D AND E)

TENDRIL REPEAT (STENCIL F)

FIG BORDER (STENCIL C)

TUMBLING LEAVES (STENCIL B)

CLEMATIS FLOWER BORDER (STENCILS A AND G)

PAINT COLOUR GUIDE

Bright pink   Deep green

Bright yellow

PAINTING A WALLPAPER DESIGN

1 Paint the background with a yellow emulsion.

2 The first stripe is a simple 180-degree turn using the same honeysuckle motif (stencil C). Measure the width of the first honeysuckle and use this as the width of your stripe. Use a spirit level to mask off one side of each stripe with low-tack tape and draw in the alignment of the tape on the stencil so that you can move it up or down.

3 Using the other stencils, repeat the above technique. The gap between the stencilled stripes should be just wider than the stecilling.

COTTAGE GARDEN

This charming association of flowers with its glorious cluster of old-fashioned honeysuckle and sweet peas could be found in any English cottage garden. With its profusion of vibrant colours, it lends itself to a bedroom setting. Include the insects – dragonflies, ladybirds and butterflies – hovering around the gooseberry bushes and you have captured the rural imagery associated with lazy summer evenings. This stencil could be used in a variety of ways – to enhance bedside tables, bedheads, lampshades, chests of drawers and mirrors.

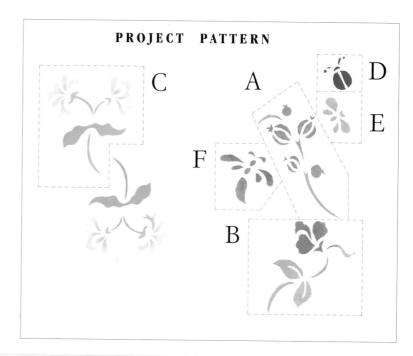

PROJECT PATTERN

CHOOSING COLOURS

Do not worry if you overlap colours or paint in unusual ones – remember that you are working with pattern and shape rather than reality. If an insect that would normally be blue turns out green, it simply adds charm to the stencilling.

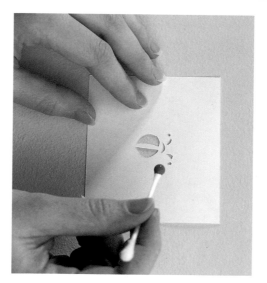

PAINTING THE INSECTS

When painting the insect stencils it is easier to apply the paint with a cotton bud to ensure you do not flood the stencil. Use it like a sponge, dab off the excess paint onto kitchen paper and then gently work it into the stencil.

EXTENDING THE THEME

One element, used as a single pattern in a room, can enhance an object and give a good visual link with the stencilled walls. Paint the object in the same way as the walls and protect it with a few layers of varnish.

COTTAGE GARDEN VARIATIONS

Paint a different garden in your bedroom – or anywhere else in the house. The simple addition of blue substantially changes the look of these motifs and you can blend colours to produce realistic-looking fruits. Use them as single images on a variety of objects and furniture or in combinations to create a country scene as a border or frieze around a room.

SIMPLE GOOSEBERRY BORDER (STENCIL A)

GOOSEBERRIES BORDER (STENCIL A)

TRAILING SWEETPEAS REPEAT (STENCIL B)

SWEETPEAS, BUTTERFLIES AND GOOSEBERRIES BORDER (STENCILS A, B AND E)

SWEETPEAS AND INSECTS MOTIF (STENCILS B, E AND F)

ENTWINED SWEETPEAS AND BUTTERFLIES (STENCILS B AND E)

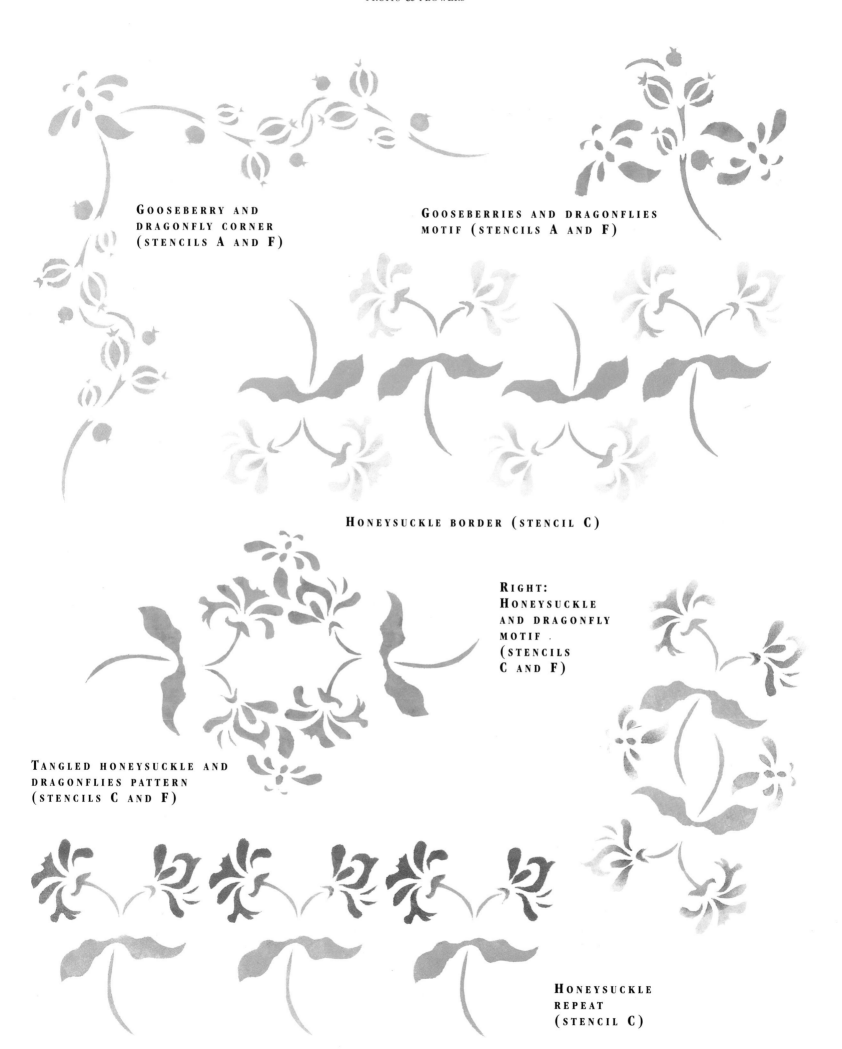

GOOSEBERRY AND DRAGONFLY CORNER (STENCILS A AND F)

GOOSEBERRIES AND DRAGONFLIES MOTIF (STENCILS A AND F)

HONEYSUCKLE BORDER (STENCIL C)

RIGHT: HONEYSUCKLE AND DRAGONFLY MOTIF . (STENCILS C AND F)

TANGLED HONEYSUCKLE AND DRAGONFLIES PATTERN (STENCILS C AND F)

HONEYSUCKLE REPEAT (STENCIL C)

SUPPLIERS

Emulsion paints are easily obtainable from DIY stores and good hardware stores; contact manufacturers below for your nearest supplier. Oil sticks and acrylic paints can be obtained from artists' materials stores. Other stencilling supplies can usually be found in any of the above and there are many dedicated stencil stores.

Imperial Chemical
Industries plc (ICI)
(Dulux paints)
Wexham Road
Slough
SL2 5DS
(Tel. 01753 550000)

Crown Decorative
Products
PO Box 37
Crown House
Hollins Road
Darwen
Lancashire
(Tel. 01254 704951)

Fired Earth plc
Twyford Mill
Oxford Road
Adderbury
Oxfordshire
(Tel. 01295 812088)

ACKNOWLEDGEMENTS

Thanks to Philippa Vereker and Katherine MacInnes for their enormous contribution to the text; to the Hudson family for their inspiration; to Tom Smail, Steph and Roy Tiley for their constant support; and finally to Karen, Colin, Clare and Graeme for their enthusiasm, patience and tolerance.

First published in 1998 by Merehurst Limited
Ferry House, 51–57 Lacy Road, Putney, London SW15 1PR

© Copyright 1998 Merehurst Limited

ISBN 1-85391-602-1

A catalogue record of this book is available from the British Library.

Edited by Geraldine Christy
Photography by Graeme Ainscough
Styling by Clare Louise Hunt

Colour separation by Bright Arts (HK) Limited
Printed in Singapore

Katrina Hall divides her time between stencilling, paint effects and interior design for both commercial projects and private clients.

SPRING LILIES & CRAB APPLES

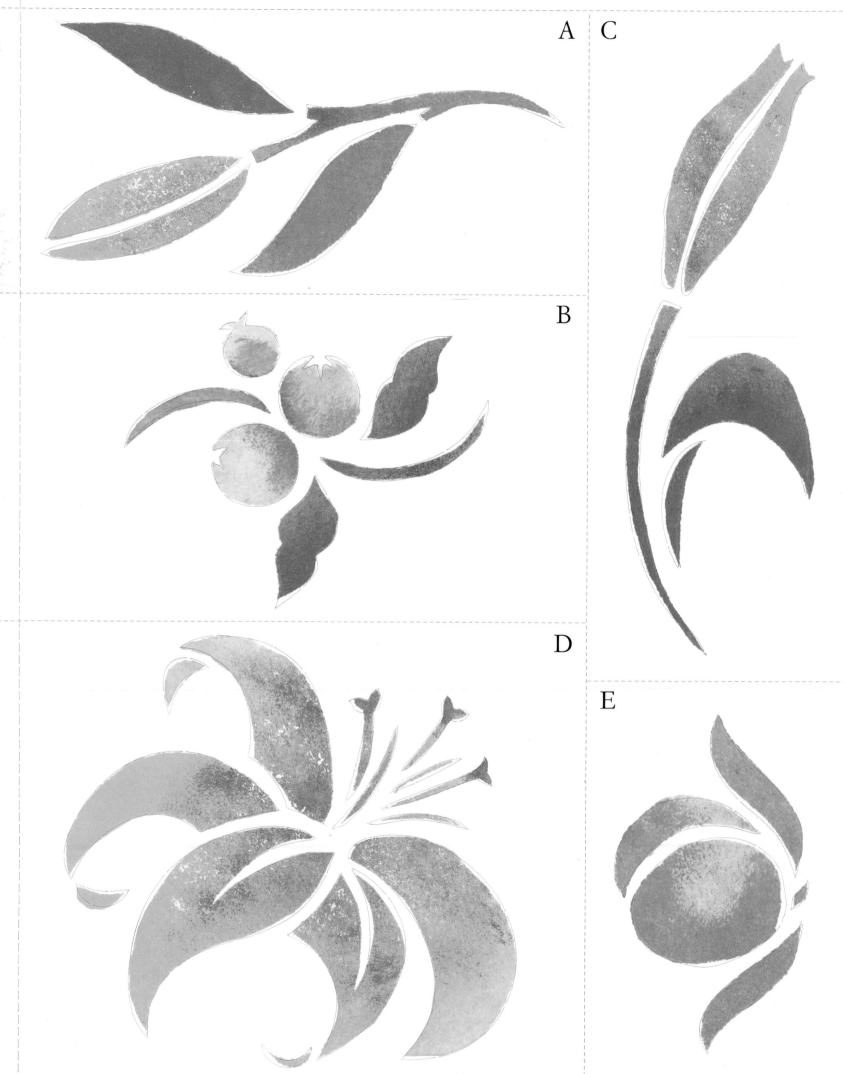

A

C

B

D

E

CHINESE POMEGRANATES

A B

C D

E F

A

B

C

D

A B

C

D E F

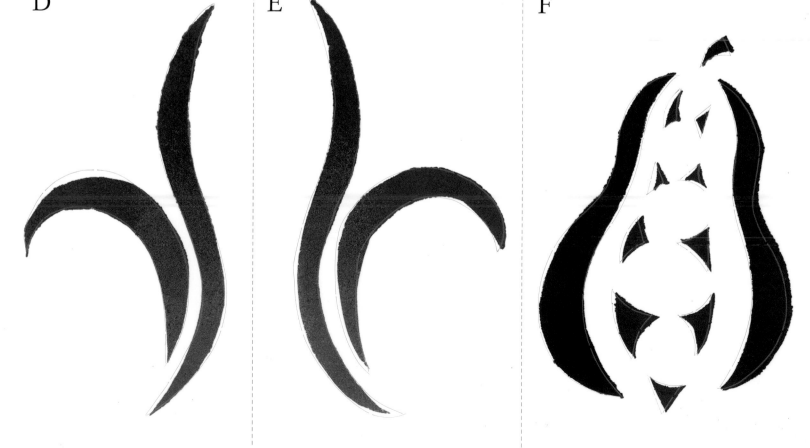

PROVENÇAL FIGS & CLEMATIS

A B

C D

E F G

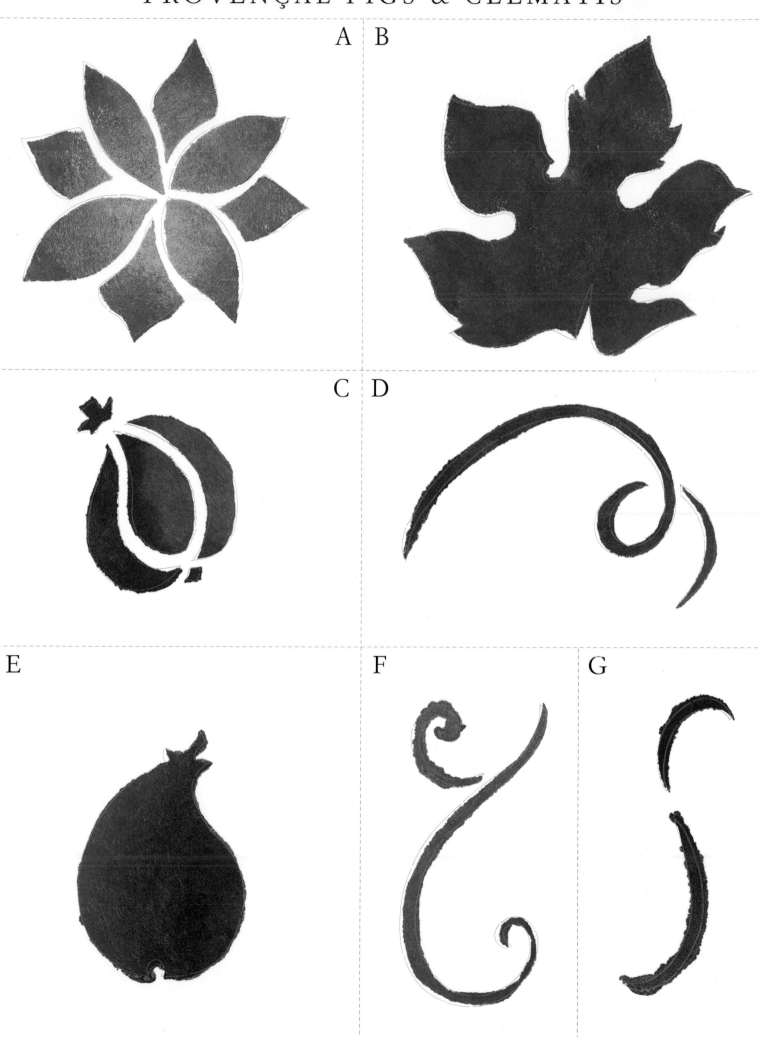

COTTAGE GARDEN

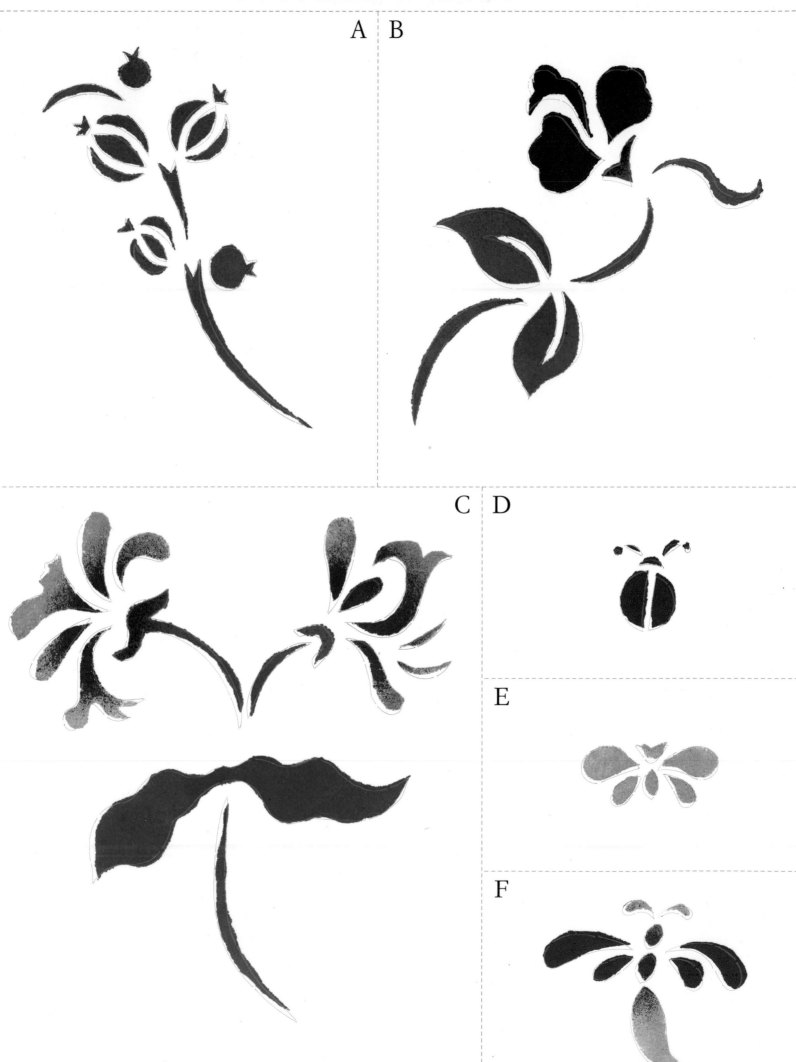

A B

C D

E

F